Teach *Me* PR 101

A Guide for the New (or not so new) Entrepreneur

who wants to Master the Basics of Public Relations for

your Brand or Business

By: *Leslie Green*

Publicist, Entrepreneur, Author

Teach Me PR 101

A Guide for the New (or not so new) Entrepreneur who wants to Master the Basics of Public Relations for your Brand or Business

•Are you a new or aspiring business owner who has no idea how to publicize yourself and build a relationship with your new clientele?

•Are you an existing business owner who is ready to take your business to the next level by developing a PR Strategy?

•Are you in business for yourself and know you need PR, but you just don't have the budget to pay someone else to do it?

If you answered yes to any of these questions, you need to master the basics of PR for your business or your brand and this book teaches you how. Many business owners, especially new ones, desperately need PR services, but they don't have the resources or bandwidth to invest in a professional who can help publicize their brands. *Teach Me PR 101* offers the basics on how to get your brand to your core audience and immediately influence them to talk about it, generating more cash flow for your business. This how to guide is designed for use with the PR 101 online course found at www.prformybusiness.com.

Author Leslie Green is the founder and CEO of Golden Life Ventures, a communications consulting agency that combines exceptional creativity with customized communication strategies to help businesses and individuals get their brand to the masses.

Printed in the United States of America

Book Cover Design/Logo: Seven Hughes, 7th Wonder
Book Editing: Natasha T. Brown, Brown and Duncan Brand, LLC
Photography: Ronald Baker, Solid Image
Print ISBN: 978-0-9984756-4-6
E-book ISBN: 978-0-9984756-5-3

Contents

Acknowledgements

First and foremost, I want to acknowledge my best friend, counselor, mentor, editor, senior intern (LOL), number one publicist, and the woman who gave me life, my momma! I say without hesitation that you are the greatest mother on this side of heaven. You have been my biggest supporter, fan, and cheerleader since the day I was born, and this project, like countless others I have birthed, could not have been done without you and your support. Thank you from the bottom of my heart for being who you are. I thank God for giving me the blessing and gift to be your daughter.

I would also like to thank Mrs. Jeneen Barlow, phenomenal life and business strategist, for hosting and executing the course that helped me birth the idea of PR 101 into the world. Your exquisite leadership, guidance, and expertise helped bring this project to fruition and your mentorship indeed encouraged me to be *more* excellent, for which I will eternally be grateful. I also want to thank my fellow Execution Revolution colleagues who gave me encouraging words of praise and feedback during the development phase of this project.

Additionally, I want to acknowledge my amazing circle of friends, colleagues, and clients who supported me from the sidelines by offering an encouraging word, praying for me, supplying additional ideas and resources, and for ultimately serving as my own PR team to help me reach every single one of you reading this book right now. I want to offer a special word of praise to my long-time dear friend, business coach, and mentor Jason Cross for his undying support and assistance at every phase of this project, from helping me conceptualize the course, down to offering feedback on the look and feel of the logo. To my whole #goldenlife tribe, you all ROCK!

Last, but certainly not least, I want to thank my Lord and Savior Jesus Christ for providing me the vision, endurance, and resources to make this all possible. Without you, I am literally nothing. To God be ALL the glory.

Making the most of
Teach *Me* PR 101

Congratulations on investing in one of the most vital components of your business – public relations (PR). If you are like most entrepreneurs or self-employed professionals, you probably didn't learn PR 101 in school. Perhaps when you launched your business, you realized that you desperately needed it. Or maybe like many, you don't even know what PR is but you know you're missing something that's holding you back from expanding your brand and developing a deeper relationship with your customer base.

Regardless of the category into which you may fall, you're in the right place. To make the most of this book, take the time to answer the questions at the end of each chapter. They will help you master the basics of each section and send you well on your way to becoming a PR pro for your business!

Okay, time for full disclosure: doing your own PR is hard work, as is the case with most things of value. Considering you are an entrepreneur, I know you are used to hard work; in fact, you may thrive off of it. But that doesn't mean you can't have fun with this. The process of learing PR comes by trial and error, and actually a few of your mistakes may lead you to some unexpected wins! So relax, and enjoy getting to know your business and clientele on a different level. It will help you tremendously in the long run.

Lastly, as you work through this book you may start to see the value in having access to template materials, case studies, worksheets, and other resources and tools that will help you along in mastering the basics of your own PR. As this book is meant to supplement the online course, PR 101, found at www.prformybusiness.com, you may want to consider investing in the full course so you can access those bonus materials.

I hope you find this information useful. And more importantly, I hope you put what you learn into action to help build and expand your enterprise. I'll see you at the top!

Chapter 1:

What is PR and Why do I need it?

What is Public Relations and Publicity?

I love the way the Public Relations Society of America defines Public Relations (PR): a strategic communication process that builds mutually beneficial relationships between organizations and their publics (or core audiences).

I like to define publicity as simply the activity or business of getting people to give attention to someone or something. The Business Dictionary states, "The main objective of publicity is not sales promotion, but creation of an image through (mostly media but also) an editorial or 'independent source' commentary."

So in a nutshell, the purpose of effective PR is to create such a great public image and trust that you get others to like and talk about you and your work in a positive way, which in turn, results in more sales and ultimately the success of your business or project.

What PR Isn't (and why it's important to not get confused)

While they have a similar end goal, PR is NOT sales or marketing or advertising. While the desired result may be to get your product or service sold, PR covers much more than that. As a PR practitioner, one's focus should be to establish a relationship with your client so that they will keep coming back to you for more value. As a business owner or brand, your focus for all of your PR efforts should be to keep your audience coming back to you to see what you are doing now and next. You want to keep them interested and engaged.

There are many companies that sell product simply because they have a great product. If they have a bad public image due to poor PR, the reality is, they probably won't be selling products for very long. Therefore, your focus as a brand cannot be to simply sell a product—no matter how enticing that goal may be. Your focus needs to be to establish brand loyalty.

Good public relations and publicity are equally as important as effective marketing and advertising strategies.

10

In fact, they work best when they are done conjointly.

Public relations is also often confused with branding. While PR professionals and branding specialists may work hand-in-hand and although their tasks overlap sometimes (i.e. identifying core audiences, developing clear messages, etc.), their end goals are different. I love how the *Small Business Chronicle* explains the difference: "In a nutshell, public relations is about managing relationships, while branding is centered on creating an identity." Branding comes before PR. If you haven't yet established the identity for your business or product, you will want to do that before you engage in PR efforts.

Why Does Any Business Need PR and Publicity Services?

You and your business image matters to your core audience. You can have a stellar brand, an amazing product, and great marketing and sales strategies to go along with it, but if you don't have great PR to enhance and maintain your image, you will not have business sustainability. Great PR and publicity supports your marketing efforts by enforcing that you are a trusted brand, others like you, and they are talking about you as well. With each positive image and message your audience receives from outside your company, the more trusted, tried, and proven you become in their eyes.

Public relations helps you engage and build a relationship with your customers. They want to support a brand that knows them and understands what they need. When you have a relationship with your customers, not only will they be loyal, they also will be vocal about their appreciation through word-of-mouth marketing. You've probably heard this before, but word-of-mouth marketing is *the best* marketing.

Types of PR Strategies

There are a number of PR strategies for business owners to consider, but for the purposes of this book, we are going to focus in on the five most popular and effective strategies used to publicize a brand and engage their audiences.

1. Grassroots/community engagement: If your product, service, or business serves the members of or requires buy-in from your local community, this PR strategy is imperative. Community engagement strategies help you build relationships with residents and fellow business owners for the purposes of uplifting and building a mutually beneficial partnership with that community.

As an example, if you own a local barbershop, you want to build relationships, not just with your potential individual clients; you will want to establish relationships with other local businesses and organizations so that you can participate in cross promotion. Many business owners get together to host neighborhood block parties (or similar programs) where they offer special promotions, giveaways, and so forth, to draw new customers and allow them to get a feel for each company's products or services. These programs also serve as great opportunities to meet and hear directly from neighboring customers and potential customers. If you are the owner of another type of storefront business, you may want to consider attending local community events. Perhaps you also may consider volunteering to speak at some of these events to increase your visibility in the community while offering your expertise in your given industry.

2. Email/Newsletter engagement: In addition to being a good sales tool, newsletters can also serve as a convenient platform to keep your customers educated and engaged. The information you provide in a newsletter can create a value-added component to the great service or product you are already giving them. Here are a few tips about establishing a good newsletter.

If you choose newsletter engagement, get yourself on a schedule so your clients will start anticipating the good content. Research shows that scheduled newsletters, verses sporadic newsletters, can be more effective in keeping your clients engaged.

Your newsletters should not be too long. Less is more. You want to give them good content that will only take a couple of minutes to read. Remember you are a competing with millions of other brands for attention, so you don't want your customer to feel overwhelmed when they open your newsletter.

Include photos to engage your readers. Research shows that content with images have a 94% higher viewer

14

rate than content without. Additionally, images have double the recall rate of text, meaning people can digest and regurgitate content better when there is an image attached to it. Therefore, if you want engaging, memorable content, include images.

3. Paid Media: Paid media is definitely a form of advertising and marketing, but it also can be a great PR tool if used effectively.

From a PR perspective, paid media is used best when you include testimonials from other people who talk about your service or product. If you acquire real live examples of how your product or service has been able to help someone, you can use that powerful testimonial in a promotion that can be disseminated widely to your core audiences. We will talk about how to get testimonials in our last chapter.

Paid media may also exist in the form of sponsorships. These also can be considered a form of community engagement. If there is a cause or non-profit organization that you can support by paying to advertise in a program or on a website that reaches your core audience, this type of paid media may be a smart PR strategy for you.

4. Traditional Earned Media: (radio, TV, newspaper and new media: podcasts and online/blogs): Earned media is just as it sounds. It cannot be bought; it has to be earned. In order to capture a media outlet's interest in writing about or featuring your project or venture, your content must be compelling, time relevant, and "newsworthy." Often times, what we as business owners believe is newsworthy is not newsworthy to the media. Therefore, it is important to know what has a good chance of being picked up (placed in the media), before you waste your time pitching stories to the media that have no chance of getting covered.

5. Social Media: Although this is certainly the newest media platform and PR tool, it has become one of the most effective and widely-used ways of publicizing a brand and engaging clients. Social media also evolves at a very fast pace. Therefore, in order to use it effectively, you must constantly be learning and open to change. You'll also want to understand which platforms make the most sense for you to focus on for your particular product or service.

These last two strategies (earned and social media) I'm going to discuss in more detail in Chapters 4 and 5, because they are the most popular and effective PR strategies for most enterprises. For a list of other PR strategies to consider for your business, refer to the resources section of the PR 101 online course at www.prformybusiness.com.

How Do You Determine What Type of PR Strategy Best Fits Your Business Model?

In the next chapter, we will talk about how to develop a communications strategy that includes the messages you want to convey to your audience and the goals/objectives of your communications strategy. The PR strategy *or strategies* that you choose will be based on the types of messages you want to convey and what your ultimate goals and objectives are. You will also consider your audience and where they are most likely to engage with you. Many communications plans utilize several types of PR strategies to cast a wide net with their core audiences. People process information differently, so you want to make sure you are meeting your customers where they are with each PR strategy you choose.

There are some other factors that also contribute to which PR strategies you choose and how to use them. These include:

•**Staffing/time:** If you are a staff of one, and are currently your own PR staff, you may want to consider holding off on earned media until you can get some help because it can be labor intensive, or perhaps you want to consider hiring someone to help you manage the pitching and fielding interview requests. Another idea is to recruit some loyal supporters to serve as your PR team to help you do the heavy lifting while you're out there doing what you do best—being creative.

•**Budget:** Consider carving out a budget within the funds you have set aside for your promotional materials to include paid media and sponsorship opportunities that will be crucial to engaging your customers. While many of your PR efforts will not require a financial investment (besides labor), as you grow, you will want to consider paying for some of the tools that will help publicize your business. As an example, there are a lot of email platforms like MailChimp, ConvertKit, Constant Contact, and AWeber that are free for a certain time period (or up to a certain amount of emails/contacts) to help distribute content to your clients. As your list grows, so will your financial investment in these types of platforms.

•**Your product/service:** If you are an independent consultant whose business is primarily online, grassroots and community engagement may not be the best strategy to engage your clientele and to publicize your services. In this case, you will want to develop an online strategy.

Questions to Ponder:

① If you are an existing business owner: Now that you have a full understanding of what PR is and what it isn't, what PR efforts have you already been doing for your business?

a. Have those efforts been effective for you so far in gaining new customers and sustaining existing customers?

b. Where can you see yourself supplementing or tweaking your current efforts with some of the strategies mentioned above?

② If you are a new business owner starting a new project or business: Does your business and/or project have a clearly defined brand identity established?

③ What is your current budget for PR/publicity?

④ If you are a team of one: Do you have the capacity to hire low-level staff such as an assistant or an intern to help you with some of your PR efforts?

⑤ If you have little-to-no budget for PR, who can you en-list to provide volunteer assistance from your support circle?

Chapter 2:

What's Your Message and Your Plan?

Why It Is Important to Have Three to Five Key Messages

The first step to developing a solid communications strategy is to figure out what important messages you want to convey to your audience. You cannot speak to your audience if you don't have clarity around what you want to say. It is also vital to develop these messages because key messages will guide every piece of communication that comes from you. Writing and speaking about yourself will become easy, because everything you say will be some type of extension of what is in those core messages.

Lastly, the more consistent and focused you are on staying on these same three to five messages, the easier it will be for people to talk about you and your brand with others and spread the word. Your core audience will know that you are the go-to girl or guy in your respective niche.

How to Determine Your Three to Five Key Messages

Create your core messages by asking yourself a series of questions:

•Who are you? If there is one sentence that describes who you are and what you do, what would that be?

•What problem does your business, project, or service address or solve?

•What is the ultimate goal of your enterprise? (Some businesses may have a similar answer from the previous question. Others may not.)

•Who are you serving and why?

•How are you different from anyone else in your field or industry?

Your messages should be defined by what I like to call the Core C's: clear, concise and consistent.

•**Be clear.** Remember the purpose of PR is to establish and build a relationship with your clients. They should not be confused about who you are and what you do. The better they understand both, the more inclined they will be to follow you and bring others along.

•**Be concise.** Long, drawn out messages are hard to understand and articulate. The more concise you are, the more people will be able to share your messages with others.

•**Be consistent.** Your messages should be consistent with your brand or your identity and they should be in alignment with your mission. No matter how you expand or evolve, your messages should be consistent with your mission.

Example: Here are a few key messages that I developed for one of my most recent clients:

Client X, a visibility and media strategist with more than 25 years' experience in television and online media and entrepreneurship, is the go-to expert for existing business owners and aspiring entrepreneurs who are looking to gain clarity and visibility for their businesses.

Client X works with corporate professionals, coaches, experts, authors, speakers, business owners, and visionaries to develop, secure, and execute an online media platform and enterprise that builds brand influence and income.

Client X offers a customized approach to coaching based

on individual needs to help clients unlock and unleash their passions and learn how to hustle in business, while loving life in the process.

What Are the Key Components of a Communications Strategy and How Do You Create One?

All communications plans are different, but most contain the basic elements. These include:

~Messages

~Goals and/or Objectives

~Audience

~Tactics

~Action Steps

We've already discussed messages. Now let's break down the other components.

•Goals and/or Objectives

Your objectives and goals are similar and should be in alignment with one another.

Your objectives are your 30,000-foot view of what you want to accomplish with this communication plan. As an example, if you own a hair salon, perhaps one of your objectives is to be known as the #1 go-to hair salon in your market for a specific type of hair care.

Your goals should be set based on how you envision meeting that objective and it should be measurable. As an example, your goal to meet that objective might be to attract 10 new customers per week via social media promotions.

I believe it's important to have both goals and objectives. Look at it like the objective is your "Why" and the goal is your "How." You cannot hit a target unless you have one, so the better you are at establishing your goals and objectives, the more successful you will be in implementing your strategy.

•**Audience**

It is important to identify who your communications plan is targeting by mapping out your audiences. Once you know who you are targeting, the people you want to reach will be much easier to find.

If you believe your audience is everyone, you will need to revisit your goals and objectives and define them a bit more. Remember the more specific you are in identifying who your audience is, the more precise you'll be in reaching that audience and gaining their business and loyalty.

Ask yourself, *who stands to benefit most from the product or service I offer?*

One of my good friends started a life coaching business. What makes her unique (her niche) is that she is not looking for any and every one. She wants to work specifically with women who are uncertain and unclear about their purpose. That's it. Very simple, but very specific. You may not have a business that is as narrow in focus as my friend's, but that does not mean you cannot target the audiences you want to attract.

•Tactics

The tactics are the meat of your plan. This is where you will need to be creative and maybe even seek some counsel from a PR professional. You may not have the finances right now to invest in a PR professional to implement your plan on a monthly retainer, but that person could help you to create that plan, or at least give you some ideas that you can implement yourself.

As we discussed in Chapter 1, you will want to develop the tactics based on the types of PR strategies that you select.

As an example, if you know social media engagement will be a key PR strategy for your business, you will need to develop tactics for implementing that social media strategy.

One way that I have been able to help my clients gain exposure with potential new followers and engage with their current followers on social media is by creating contests. People love trivia, competition, and more importantly, FREE stuff. If you have some promotional materials to give away, including hats, t-shirts, magnets, CDs, you can offer them as prizes for the winners of your contest. These promotional items may come at a nominal cost to you, but could make the difference between a one-time customer and a lifelong loyal client. You can also tie in a stipulation for the contest to like, follow, or share your page or posts. That will have a double effect of creating good will and growing your visibility. That is an example of a tactic within your social media engagement PR Strategy.

For a breakdown of more PR tactics in a case study, refer to Module 2 of the PR 101 online course at www.prformybusiness.com.

•Action Steps

Your action steps are what put your plan into motion. Your action steps keep you on task. It's best if your action steps come with a timeline attached to them so you can see your progress and keep yourself accountable in meeting your goals. It doesn't even necessarily have to be a hard and fast date; you could have a general timeframe such as a month as a deadline. Additionally, your action steps should be just as specific and measurable as your goals are.

Example: PR Plan Timeline

Month	Press Strategy	Action Step	Status
January	Press Release Distribution	Begin plan for regular press release distribution	Completed
January	Social Media Engagement	Ramp up activity on social media platforms. Add new features and engaging followers/ group members with interesting dialogue	Ongoing
February	Director Listening Tour	Attend and host regular events and meetings with main constituent groups	Ongoing
March	Paid Advertising	Design a strategic advertising plan that promotes services and features of agency to audiences	In progress

Questions to Ponder:

① Who are the core audiences you would like to reach? In other words, who are your customers and desired customers?

② Where can you find your core audiences?

③ What are the goals and objectives of your PR/communications plan?

④ What messages do you want to convey to your core audiences?

⑤ What PR strategies best fit your goals and objectives?

TEACH ME PR 101

Chapter 3:

How to Earn Media Part 1

What is Earned Media?

Earned media means gaining the attention of traditional news outlets (print, radio, TV and now new media including podcasts and blogs) typically by making a "pitch" for them to cover/attend or write a story on your event, project, or service. As mentioned in Chapter 1, earned media is just as it sounds. It cannot be bought; it has to be earned. When you really get good at what you do, sometimes you won't even have to make a pitch…they'll come to you!

In order to gain the media outlet's interest with your pitch, your content must be compelling, time relevant, and "newsworthy." As mentioned previously, often times, what we as business owners believe is newsworthy is not necessarily newsworthy, in the eyes of the media. Therefore, take some time to consider whether or not your content is compelling enough to be considered "news" to the general public.

When you have compelling content, there are some clever tactics and enticing language you can use to make your idea stand out among the crowded field of competitors. We'll go over some of these tactics when we discuss the pitch.

How Do I Know If My Content Is Compelling Enough to Attract the Media?

Here are some questions to ask yourself and/or a trusted counselor or friend before you develop your pitch:

• What would an ideal story about what I'm pitching say?

• Is what I'm pitching unique? If it is, how so?

• Would I read an article or listen to or watch a story about that?

• Is what I'm pitching time-sensitive/relevant?

• Why would the media be inclined to publish/broadcast my content?

• What will readers, listeners, viewers gain by accessing this content?

If you were able to answer the questions and they are satisfactory to you, move forward to the next step. If they are not, you may need some fine tuning before you make your pitch. You might also want to consider doing a small focus group with some trusted colleagues to learn how your idea lands on them, before moving forward. If "now" is not the right time for media outreach, don't force it. There are other ways to gain free publicity for your work, until you have something really newsworthy to pitch.

How to Build a Media List

First you need to know who you are targeting. This step can be the hardest part of the process because building a media list can be very time consuming and requires a lot of research. The good news is, once you have built your list, you don't have to build it again, from scratch anyway. [Important note: You might need to update this list every quarter or so, because the media industry has a high turnover rate and reporters often change or rotate the "beats" or topics they cover.] If you have a budget, there are also companies that you can hire to build targeted media lists and even send out press releases on your company's behalf. For a detailed list of the best companies for these services, refer to Module 3 of www.prformybusiness.com.

Print

    For local coverage, start with the major outlets that you know and patronize. For example, if you live in Atlanta, start with the *Atlanta Journal Constitution* and find the section of the paper where you would most likely see a story similar to what you are pitching. For instance, if you are a gifted artist and you want this outlet to cover the grand opening of your new collection or gallery, you would want to go the Art/Lifestyle section. If your event, project, or service is community based, reach out to a community newspaper. These publications are short-staffed and may require multiple calls and/or emails, but they may be a perfect outlet for the type of story you want to pitch.

    If your business, project, or event lends itself to national coverage, you want to begin to build a list of major national outlets and take the same type of approach in terms of narrowing down your target to the section of the paper that corresponds to your area of expertise. *Note: One of the* *biggest mistakes brands make is pitching their stories to outlets that are not interested and do not cover their industry or service. As enticing as it may be, <u>do not</u> pitch your local-focused story to a national news outlet or your music/arts story to a business or sports reporter. This is the quickest way to end up in the "Spam" folder.*

Next, investigate who has written articles similar to your ideal article, and then add that journalist to your list. You will also want to put the editor (or producer, for television) of that section on your list as well, because those are the decision makers for the stories that get selected to run. You can find some reporters and editors' contact information in a hyperlink of their name in an article they wrote online. If it is hyperlinked, simply right click to copy and paste the email. Other smaller papers may have a Staff page with contact information on their website. If you aren't able to find their information on the website, you can call the general number and ask for that reporter or editor's email address. If you have to call, make sure you have your elevator pitch ready, because they may ask you what you want to send, before they give you an email address.

Radio & TV

Radio and television work a little differently than print and online publications. Often times, you will find very little-to-no information about staff members on a new station's website. For TV, you may need to go through the general news desk to get anything on their radar. The good news is, when you send an email to a general email address like newsdesk@fox5wkpi.com, it goes to a number of reporters and editors at once so you're able to have multiple eyes on your work, thus multiple opportunities for a "yes." The bad news is that you and everyone else are sending their story ideas to the general inbox, so you may need to follow up multiple times to get some traction.

For radio, each station runs slightly different. First, you want to identify what target markets you are going after so that you can narrow down the options to research. For instance, most music radio stations have a talk component to them, so you should refer to your target audiences and research the radio stations based upon the audiences that each station targets. If your target market is African-American young adults between the ages of 18 and 25, you will definitely want to go after urban radio stations versus talk radio stations. If your event is one that will involve some type of community engagement, call and see if there is a community or public affairs person to get your foot in the door that way. *Note: Many radio stations offer free/unpaid air time for public affairs PSAs (public service announcements) for non-profit organizations.*

New Media

Online media and publications such as blogs and YouTube channels are the newest forms of media, but often times they can have the most reach, because they are not bound by geographical limitations. Again, depending on your target audiences, this may be the best approach to receive earned media, especially in the beginning stages of your plan. As an example, if your business, project, or event has a target audience of young mothers with children from infants to elementary school aged children, you definitely want to have prominent mommy blogs at the top of your media list. You will get the most bang for your buck impressions-wise with new media.

41

As you are building and refining your list, there are some important facts to remember:

•Your list will never be complete. It will always be a working, living, breathing document. There will be some trial and error in fine-tuning your target media list. With that in mind, if you come across someone who is just not the right fit at all for your type of story, it's always helpful to ask if there is someone else at the outlet with whom they can connect you. More often than not, journalists are helpful and can steer you to another reporter that may be interested.

•Try to get as many email addresses AND direct phone numbers as possible. That way if you can't reach someone one way, you can reach them through another form of communication, and you won't have to go back online to do the research, in the middle of your pitching process.

•It may sound counterintuitive, but the more narrow and focused you are in building your media list, the better chance you will have of getting someone to cover your brand. People often have an urge to add every single outlet on a media list, hoping that whatever they throw at it will stick. However, the truth is, you'll waste your time if you are pitching outlets or reporters that will never pick up your story.

•Use your contacts. Ask around your network to see if your contacts have any relationships in the media. Find out if they are willing to share your story with their media contacts. This will at least get your foot in the door and put you a step above everyone else who is submitting a pitch the traditional way. Remember, effective PR is all about managing relationships. Why not use them when you can!

Questions to Ponder:

① Do you have any newsworthy content to share?

② Based onyour content, is traditional or new media better to pitch or should you pitch both?

③ What outlets do you currently patronize that share similar content about your business, product, or service?

④ What outlet has produced a similar type of story or television/radio spot?

⑤ Do you know anyone who has contacts in the media?

TEACH ME PR 101

Chapter 4:

How to Earn Media Part 2

How to Write a Press Release and Media Advisory

Let us first cover the difference between a media advisory and a press release.

A media advisory (or media alert) is a concise document giving a bulleted who, what, when, and where description of an event you are promoting that you would like the media to cover or attend. This document is emailed or faxed at least a week out from the event and gives just enough information to pique the reporter's interest in covering the story.

A press release is an announcement or summary of news intended for use by the media to write their own story or publish as written. A press release, if used in conjunction with a media advisory, is typically sent the day of or day after the event has transpired to give a longer, detailed explanation of what is being announced for the media to include in a story. You can also have the press release ready to hand out in person to any media who cover the event as background information.

There is also an embargoed press release that is used when you want to give a reporter or outlet advance information on your announcement with the understanding that they are not to publish any information from the release until the embargo is released. The advantage to the reporter or outlet is that they will have first mover's advantage to publish because they had time to prepare the body of their story and can immediately publish the story the moment the embargo is lifted. In the news business, timing is everything and if an outlet can have the news first, you've just earned a friend in addition to a story. Historically, this tactic has been used for established brands or personalities (such as celebrity figures or well-known businesses) and there is a demand on the information being released. For instance, news about the latest Apple iPhone details or the birth of a celebrity child of pop culture icons like Kim Kardashian and Kanye West, might call for an embargoed press release. However, as the media industry has changed over the years, giving embargoed or exclusive rights to a story is becoming more of a widely-accepted practice by established and un-established brands.

A press release can have many functions that include:

~To make an announcement about an event

~To share new information about a new business, project, or idea

~To promote a product or service

If you are making an announcement about an event that you want the media to attend or "cover," it is best to lead with a media advisory, so that you don't give them too much up-front information. If they get too much information before-hand it will give them less of a reason to attend.

Your media advisory should have the following components:

•**What:** Two to three sentences giving a description of what the event will announce or unveil.

•**Who:** Who are the big players involved? If there are any notable attendees, list them first.

•**When:** Give the date and time of event (including press check-in time, which is typically earlier than the start time, especially for TV outlets, which will need extra time to set up).

•**Where:** Give the location and any pressing details regarding where the media should park.

•**Contact Info:** Who should the media contact to RSVP or reach the day of the event, for last minute requests or information?

Your press release should have the following components:

•**Letterhead/Logo** (optional)**:** If you have a logo, you should use it. Your branding adds credibility to what you are sharing in the release and makes your releases easily identifiable. You can use your logo for the media advisory as well.

•**Date Line:** This is the date your announcement is being released to the public. [For Immediate Release: October 19, 2016]

•**Contact Information:** This is extremely important, because the media needs to know who they should reach in case they need more information. You should provide a contact name, phone number and email address of whoever you want to handle media calls. That person may or may not be you.

•**Headline:** If you are sending your release via email, as most pitches are, this headline will be the first thing the media sees so it needs to be compelling and concise. Some of these reporters, editors, and news desks receive dozens, and sometimes hundreds, of emails per day. You want your release to stand out from the crowd. The most eye-catching part of your event should be included in this headline. As an example, if you have someone well-known coming to your event, that person's name should be in the headline. Also, if you have a national focus, but you are speaking to a particular market, you should include that market's name in the headline (i.e. Breakthrough Beauty Formula for Denver Women Revealed).

•**Sub-headline** (optional): The sub-headline just simply explains the headline in more detail. A sub-headline to compliment the headline above may read: *Color Me Lovely beauty line to launch this weekend at downtown Sephora Store*

•**Lead paragraph:** This first paragraph of your release should briefly give an overview of whatever it is you are announcing. Because media professionals are reading a number of these per day, it is important to get to the point of what you are announcing right away and give them enough information to determine whether or not they want to cover it in that lead paragraph. This paragraph should be no longer than two or three sentences.

•**Body:** The rest of the release should give supporting information to what you shared in the lead paragraph. It can include quotes from the major players and go further into detail of what it is you are announcing. Your quotes should be the only part of your release expressing an opinion. The rest of the release should include only facts, as some outlets may want to publish your news release as written.

•**Boilerplate language about person/project/company:** This language will appear at the bottom of every release and provide general information about your company or project and its mission. It may be up to four sentences and include a website for more information. *Note: Try to keep your press release one page (front). Less is more in media pitching.*

For an example of a media advisory and press release that lead to local and national media coverage, refer to Module 4 of the PR 101 online course at www.prformybusiness.com.

How to Write a Pitch Email

A pitch email is a personalized email intended to sell an idea to the media or persuade them to interview someone or cover an event. This is used as an alternative method to sending out a blast press release, and while it may be more time consuming, it can generally lead to more favorable results than a blast press release. Pitch emails are targeted and personalized based upon your knowledge of a reporter and/or outlet. It can use components of the press release but it is not as formal and should be tailored to what the particular media outlet or reporter covers.

Like press releases, pitch emails should have a compelling headline and the first paragraph should sum up what you are asking and why they should pay attention to it. Pitch emails should be concise and get straight to what you are asking the media to do.

The pitch email should be addressed to a specific person. The media gets tons of press releases, and advisories, and everything else you can imagine, so when something is addressed specifically to them, they are more likely to spend a couple more seconds looking through your email. All you need is a couple more seconds anyway because your email should be brief, but compelling and should have a call to action.

A call to action for media could include:

~Covering an event

~Interviewing someone

~Writing a story about the announcement you're making

For an example of a pitch email, refer to Module 4 of the PR 101 online course at www.prformybusiness.com.

How to Make a Pitch Call

For the reasons mentioned previously, some reporters require a personal follow-up before they confirm whether or not they will cover your story or interview you or your colleague. The pitch call has the same purpose as the pitch email, but you must be even more concise.

In most cases, your pitch call should be a follow-up to a pitch email or a press release you have already sent. After your initial greeting, "[Hello my name is X, and I'm calling on behalf of Y…]" use the same language you used in the headline or lead paragraph of your pitch email or press release. In some cases, the person may say, "Yes I did see something about that." In most cases, the reporter will not remember your email, so if they do not acknowledge seeing your pitch, assume they didn't get it, and move on to your call-to-action.

A pitch call may sound like this:

*Hi my name is Sam Williams, and I'm calling on behalf of The Greenhouse Foundation. I'm calling to follow-up on an email I sent regarding an unprecedented grant the foundation is making to the West Key High School there in San Diego to help prepare their students for college. **[Pause for them to speak. Whether they acknowledge receiving or not, proceed.]** This is going to help a lot of San Diego high school students, and I know your readers would love to hear about this. Would you be able to come or send someone else* *to the press announcement on Tuesday at 10 am at the school to get the breaking details of this exceptional grant program?*

If you do not get a positive response to your pitch call, find out if there is someone better suited to cover the event or story.

If you get a voicemail greeting, my recommendation is not to waste your time leaving a message. People in general, much less reporters, do not check voicemail much anymore. If they do happen to check it, the likelihood of them being compelled enough to pick up the phone to call you back is slim. My advice for you is to hang up, and call him/her back until they answer.

Questions to Ponder:

① What is your call-to-action for the pitch email or call?

② Do you need a media advisory or a press release, or both?

③ What is the most compelling part about what you're pitching?

④ What is your elevator speech for your business, product, or service?

⑤ Would you cover the story you are pitching if you were a reporter?

Chapter 5:

How to Leverage Social Media

Why Use Social Media as a PR Strategy?

In today's society, no matter what background, age, ethnic group, or gender you are targeting, the one common place you can find all of these groups is on social media. If you want to be effective at PR, you need to meet your audience where they are, and most of your audience is online.

Remember that social media has no geographical boundaries or limitations, so it can be extremely efficient and effective. You can build relationships with as many people as you want and publicize your business with one click of a button. Often times, it is free...which brings me to my next point...

Social media is a phenomenal publicity tool because of the value and traction you will receive compared to the cost that you invest. You are able to reach hundreds, thousands, and when you're really good, millions of people for a nominal cost. In addition, I would highly recommend on-line advertising to help target and reach your key audiences.

How to Determine Which Platforms to Use

Often times, the biggest question entrepreneurs are faced with is what social media platforms they should use to promote their business. The obvious ones for most businesses to utilize are Facebook with nearly 2 billion monthly active users, Instagram with more than 500 million users, and Twitter with close to 320 million monthly active users (as of December 2016). The ways you use each of them may differ from business to business, but there are some general tricks of the trade with each one from which any business can benefit. In addition, if you are looking to reach a younger audience, you may want to consider Snapchat.

In addition, you want to try to incorporate one live video streaming service within your marketing or publicity plan. Examples are Periscope and Facebook Live, which will help individuals who have personal brands or focused on teaching, coaching, or building an international audience (or businesses that depend heavily on online sales).

For the purposes of this book, I will focus my attention on the first three listed above. That is not to say that your business shouldn't be on the other platforms. In fact, LinkedIn is another platform that I highly recommend for business owners, especially if you have a business-to-business (B2B) sales model.

Do's and Don'ts—Tricks of the Trade in Social media

A common question that I receive from business owners, especially solopreneurs, is whether or not they should launch a business profile in addition to their personal social media accounts. The answer is a resounding YES! There are a few reasons for this.

•Some posts will be appropriate for both of your pages. In fact, it is a good practice to cross promote on your business and personal accounts because:

•Your friends on your personal account will have access to what you are doing business-wise and will follow your business page and/or promote it to their networks, if there is good content there.

•Your business account followers can see the personal side of you as the business owner and your brand; it humanizes the business.

•For many people, an organization's website is a second or third stop after they visit a Facebook or Instagram profile that interests them. If you have a business profile on the social media platform of your audience's choice, it legitimizes the business for them in a way. It will also educate your audience on the services you offer or products that you sell. Your social media will direct them to your website for more information and perhaps to purchase. Cross promotion amoung your personal and business accountants as well as across social media platforms assists with the goal of meeting your customers where they are.

•You can integrate your social media business profiles, particularly Facebook and Twitter, with your website via plugins. This is a good idea because it will drive eyes to your social media profiles, and since those platforms are instantaneous, you add more value and provide a way for people to get to know your business beyond (sometimes static) content on a website. Additionally, the more attention your Facebook profile receives, the more traffic your website will receive.

EVERYTHING You Do and Say Online Matters

You are your business. This point is especially true if you are cross promoting between your personal and business profiles, which I highly recommend.

Even if the two profiles are separate, your followers judge your business based on what you say on either profile. Some may argue that it isn't fair, but that's just the way it works. Once you become a business owner, even your personal profiles become fair game for business scrutiny, so you always have to be careful about what you post and how it may affect your brand. Each time you prepare to post a comment on social media, ask yourself: *Will this help or hurt my brand? Will this post help to build or tear down my relationship with my followers?* **Every post has the potential to do one or the other.**

This does not mean that every post on your personal page should be about your business or have some tie-in for your business. In fact, if you do that, you might as well just call your personal profile your business profile. Again, it's good to post personal things about yourself, because it humanizes you, but just know that all eyes watching are not really just your "friends," they are consumers of your brand as well.

Post Consistently, but Don't Consistently Post the Same Things

Repetition is the mother of learning, but there is nothing more annoying than seeing the same advertisement over and over again, especially when it wasn't particularly moving in the first place. Those are grounds to get unfollowed.

Posting consistently is important, because it keeps you relevant and at the top of your audiences' mind, but if you want to build a relationship with them and keep them coming back, you need to constantly add value while continuing to emphasize your core messages. Yes, this will require some time for you to be creative, but it will be worth it.

Here are some recommendations for adding value and being creative, while staying consistent to your messages:

•**Pictures say a thousand words.** This statement is

now more true than ever in the social media-driven society in which we live. As we talked about in Chapter 1 regarding images in newsletters, visually stimulating content like photos are always sure to gain attention and add value. According to the highly successful business and marketing blog *Quicksprout,* images are the number one most important factor in optimizing social media content.

•**Engage your audience with questions.** When building relationships on any platform, it is important to get to know your audience. Do this by asking questions. Polling your audience encourages them to interact with you and your page. Your questions should not sound like an interrogation, rather a conversation. You should also ask open-ended questions so they can insert their own thoughts. As an example, if you are in the travel business a great question to ask is, "If you could go anywhere in the world, and time and money were no issue, where would you go?"

•**Share like-minded posts.** Sharing posts from your audience and/or posts from non-competing businesses that speak to the same audience will not only create good will, it will ultimately drive more potential followers to your page. When you share others' content, they will naturally want to share yours (especially when it's helpful) and that will in turn make your page visible to followers in their network.

•**Comment and like other people's posts.** There is something about reciprocity that works wonders for brands. When you like and comment on others' posts, they will naturally return the favor…and their "friends" or followers will see your posts too. An added bonus is even if they don't share your posts in return, when you like, or, better yet, comment on a post after others have commented on it, particularly on Facebook, you stand the chance of other people in their network seeing your comment. This will help you recruit more followers, by simply being "social."

Facebook Page vs. Facebook Group

Another frequent question that I receive is, "*Should I create a Facebook Group or a Facebook Page?* There are pros and cons to both, and it really depends on your business type, company message, and your purpose for using

Facebook.

Facebook Page

A Facebook Page is essentially a profile for your business. The creator or administrator of the page has sole control over the content. It is more informational in nature and the business owner can invite their audience to "like" the page. Any content that you post ideally *may* show up in the news feed of anyone who follows the page, but it will not be displayed with the same frequency as posts by their followers.

Pros

•You control the content that is being disseminated, so you will manage the message to your audience.

•You can use Facebook advertising to target users that you want to attract.

•Pages (as with personal profile pages) can have customizable URLs, and you can promote the page to fans easily and directly.

•"Facebook Insights" is available for pages to help you understand the statistics of your page and how to optimize content.

•You can automate Facebook Page posts and send posts from other apps such as Instagram directly to Facebook, without being logged into the app. With pages, you can also sync your posts with a Twitter page, so that any content that you post on Facebook will go to Twitter as well. This is oftentimes a helpful strategy for new social media users.

Cons

•When you are first building your page, it is hard to get likes or even eyes on a post without investing in advertising, because the likelihood of your post showing high up in your followers' news feeds is slim. This is because Facebook changes its algorisms frequently, so posts from your page that have a high engagement rate will appear more frequently. In addition, unlike a group, the members will not receive an alert when you post. The only way followers will see it is if they are consistently going to your page for new content, or it happens to show up in their news feed on Facebook, or from third-party apps, such as a website plugin.

•It takes time to build the page by promoting it organically. You will need patience and buy-in from your target audience to share your posts with their networks. You will also need to be thinking of and posting content constantly to drive interest.

•This is a pro and a con: Pages are public, so anyone can see the content. Now this is a positive because you *want* as many eyes on your page as possible, but this also means that it will be more difficult to manage your audience or even their comments and messages as you grow. *Note: The latter is obviously a good "problem" to have.*

Facebook Group

A Facebook Group is more of a forum and communications tool where anyone who joins the group has the ability to post and share content. It is therefore run by the community of members. The owner of the page often functions merely as a facilitator or moderator and has provided members with a certain level of control. All members of the group will receive an alert when content is posted there, and it will show up in their newsfeeds (unless they mute alerts from the page).

Pros

•The likelihood of your members seeing what you post is very high, because they will receive an alert from Facebook whenever someone posts in the group.

•Groups give your audience more of an opportunity to connect with each other and you because it drives communication between each party. As time passes, camaraderie is created among your group members that cannot be duplicated in another type of platform.

•Groups lend themselves more to word-of-mouth marketing, as group members can invite their friends to join the group and the conversation.

•As the manager of a group, you do not have to think as much about content, because your members are posting it for you once the community is built.

•You can create events for your group and automatically invite and communicate with everyone. (Whereas, with pages, you have to individually invite others' to events created there and it can be very time consuming.)

Cons

•You do not have control over what your members post. You can always delete an inappropriate comment, but your group members receive an alert immediately when someone posts, so damage could be done before you have a chance to react to it. This leads to my next point.

•Facebook Groups can be time consuming if you want to control and police what's happening in the group. If you have the type of business where clear rules and expectations need to be set for what to post or not to post, then you (or someone you designate to manage that group) will have to monitor the content several times a day to be sure everyone is following the rules. As an example, if one of the rules is that the members are not allowed to advertise their own businesses, someone should be there to monitor and discipline the offender immediately when that type of behavior takes place.

•For business purposes, it's hard to monitor statistics for your group, because Facebook Insights is not available for groups.

•Unless someone invites a new member, most groups

71

are much harder for your audience members to find on their own, depending on the privacy setting. Again, this also depends on the purpose of your group; you may want your group to be closed or secret, in which case you don't want your group to be found by random outsiders.

I love the questions Jeannie Chan at CauseVox asks to help determine which option is best for a business or if perhaps both are good for different purposes:

•Do you want to use Facebook to make announcements and updates about your organization?

•Do you want to primarily produce your own content and post updates?

•Do you want to establish an official, public presence for your organization?

•Do you have a community who is yearning for a place to connect with each other, to have discussions with each other?

•Do you want your Facebook platform to be mostly populated by member content?

•Do you want to establish a friendly image of your organization to your supporters?

TEACH ME PR 101

If the answers to the first three questions are yes, you may want to start a Facebook Page. If the answers to the last three questions are yes, you may want to start a Facebook Group. Either option can be used effectively as a PR tool.

Social Media Advertising

Social media advertising has become one of the cheapest and fastest ways to market your business online. I won't delve deeply into social media advertising, because it is used primarily as a marketing tool but I do want to break down three of the most effective ways it can be effectively used as a PR tool.

•**Targeting media outlets and blogs in your ad.** If you target specific media for newsworthy content that you advertise, you will have a good chance of having your story placed by press. In some ways, social media advertising can be even more effective than traditional pitching, because you are attracting media with bait on a platform where they are already looking for content.

•Using ads for your posts that give away free information. Everyone loves free, especially when they believe they're getting value. If you have taken the time to create and distribute useful tips, you want as many people as possible to see it, including those who are not already following you. This will help you attract new followers and continue to add value to those who are already following you. Also, if it's really good content, people will share it, which in turn will produce more eyes on your page and potentially atrract new loyal followers.

•Ask questions and have a call to action in your ad. When you ask questions you include your audience in the conversation and encourage them to engage with you. Your followers don't want to be marketed to all of the time. You are creating a relationship with them, so if they feel included in the conversation (and the decision-making process), they will pay attention to you more often. Also giving them a call-to-action in the ad such as, "Share this if you agree," not only includes them in the conversation, but it also encourages them to include their network in the con-

74

versation as well, which expands your audience base.

Questions to Ponder:

(1) What social media platforms are you currently using for your business, and have they been effective so far in helping to build and sustain relationships with your clients?

(2) Have you consistently been using social media as a PR tool?

(3) What platforms are you not using that should be a part of your strategy?

(4) What type of free information, resources, tools, or promotional items can you give away via your social media platforms?

(5) How can you enlist your network to help you more with social media engagement?

Chapter 6:

Who do you know?
The Power of Relationships

Why Relationship Building Matters to your PR Strategy

Remember the definition of PR: a strategic communication process that builds mutually beneficial relationships between organizations and their publics (or core audiences). In order for you to build a mutually beneficial relationship between you and your core audiences, you have to get out there and spend time with them. You have to understand who they are, what they like, and where you can meet them. I don't necessarily mean in the physical sense of having in-person meetings with them, though that may be important to your strategy too. What I mean is, if your potential or future clients are African-American women between the ages of 25 and 40, you might want to start developing relationships with organizations that are comprised of those core audiences like sororities, civic and women's organizations, like Jack & Jill and Links, and the newest phenomenon – black female travel clubs. If you have a B2B product or service, joining your local chambers of commerce is critical. Once you have built relationships, selling your product or service to them will be easy, because they already know, trust, and like you.

Research Target Audiences and Questions to Ask While Building Relationships

Researching your client base is not just critical for your sales strategy, it's also critical for your PR strategy. If you really want to know and understand your target audience fully, you have to research them. In addition to learning where many of them congregate, you want to understand the diversity within that group, what motivates them to move or take action, and what do they like. Learning this information will help you bring more value to their lives and/or businesses.

The best way to research and understand your clients is to ask questions. Whether you get this information via social media, email newsletters, surveys, or in one-on-one interaction, here are some general questions that will help you understand your core audiences better:

80

•What problems do you currently face and/or what are your biggest challenges?

•Are your needs currently being met by another organization/product/service?

•What do you value most [in this type of business – barber, restaurant, accountant, etc.]?

•How do you receive your information?

•How do you like to communicate/what forums do you use?

•What and who are important to you?

•What are your annual earnings? (provide a range of options)

•What drives you to make purchasing decisions?

•How does my product/service/business help you?

•How do you prefer to shop? (online vs. in person)

Schedule Time for Relationship Building Activities

Many business owners fail at planning networking opportunities. It may not be one of the most exciting things to do, but it is one of the most important. Networking is not just about meeting new people. It's about building and maintaining relationships with the existing network you have as well.

When you are invited to functions where you know your customers or potential customers are going to be, you should make every effort to attend. This may sound very basic, and like it should be common sense, but you would be surprised how many business owners have failed at this, because they *don't feel like it* or believe they don't have time to "socialize."

Additionally, the key to good networking is to go to these events alone. Some business owners, who may be on the shy side tend to take a friend or spouse with them to these networking opportunities for moral support. Those moral supporters end up being a crutch they lean on instead of engaging with new people. If you take someone with you for support, you will inevitably spend your time talking to them rather than meeting new people.

One way to build relationships with your clients if they are in different markets is to invite them to hangouts or Q&A forums online. This doesn't have to be a weekly or even monthly event, but if it is consistent, your clients will look forward to those moments when they have an opportunity to directly engage and interact with you.

Host Customer Appreciation Events

While many businesses use customer appreciation events as a sales strategy to keep customers coming back, it is also a good PR strategy, because it is absolutely all about nurturing that relationship with your client and making him or her feel special and appreciated. Your clients also get to network with other like-minded individuals and build lasting and beneficial relationships with one another, which is another added value.

These events should not be designed just to offer your clients something for free, which is great and will keep them coming back, it's also about getting to know them and interacting with them on a more personal level. This type of relationship building activity works best when the target market is in the same location of the business. However, that's not to say that you can't get creative with technology and host "virtual" customer appreciation events, depending on the type of business you have.

Building Relationships with Journalists

If one of your core audiences is the media and you are using media relations as a PR strategy, it will become important to build relationships with journalists who cover the type of work that you do. Once you have identified who those media contacts are and you have a solid media list, you want to make sure you follow them on social media, become familiar with their work, and engage with them through Twitter, Facebook, Instagram, etc. Following them on as many platforms as possible and sharing their stories will not just help you build a relationship and good will with them, it will help you gain an understanding of the types of stories they cover and their storytelling style.

It is important to find out what the journalist wants and needs and how best you can provide it to them in a timely manner. As an example, if you've read previous stories, and you know they frequently provide quotes from multiple sources, you want to have a list of quotes ready for them from your company and also contact information for others they may want to interview as well for a balanced story. Newsrooms are severely understaffed and reporters are often times covering multiple stories at once, so the easier you can make their work for them, the more they will love you for it. And they'll keep coming back for more great content.

Questions to Ponder:

(1) Where are your core audiences? Online, social media groups, networking events, trade shows, etc?

(2) How can you get better connected to your core audiences?

(3) What invitations should you start to accept to build relationships with key groups?

(4) What questions can you ask your clients via social media, newsletters, and personal engagement to get a better understanding of them?

(5) What steps can you take right now to build a better relationship with your customer base?

Chapter 7:

How to Talk About Yourself Without Talking About Yourself

The Power of Testimonials

It is one thing for you to say great things about your business, but it's another thing entirely to have an unbiased third party say great things about your business. The purpose of a testimonial is to get others to talk about how great you are, without you having to do it. As you start to grow your business, you will find that people are happy with your product or service. One mistake business owners make is not capturing how our satisfied customers feel about us and including it in our promotional materials.

Most people do not like bragging on themselves. In fact, it can be downright uncomfortable. However, when you have an opportunity for someone else to brag on you, you should use it to your advantage. Think about a new movie release. Think about how powerful it is to have several popular and highly respected movie critics publish comments like, "Riveting," "Best romantic comedy of the year," "You won't want to stop watching!" Those are simply testimonials at work! These "critic reviews" generate word-of-mouth buzz. Remember what we said about word-of-mouth marketing right...?

If you use testimonials correctly, you won't have to work so hard at convincing others that your product or service works, because your clients will do the heavy lifting for you. There are some small businesses that have no paid advertising at all, and they have no *need* to do a significant amount of marketing or publicity, because they are booked with clients from simply referrals from their networks of past clients and their brand's social media presence.

How to Get Testimonials

The best way and time to acquire testimonials is personally asking your clients for them, immediately after they have had a good experience with your product or service. As an example, if you have a speaking business and you have just spoken at an event for your client, immediately after the event, while you are still in their presence, ask them if they will provide you with a quote about your speech, preferably on camera. That way you can use their quote in a variety of platforms (i.e. print ads, video on website, and audio on radio spots).

Another fun way of capturing testimonials is to ask your clients to send in their own videos. You can even make it a contest if you really want to stir up some excitement. This is a great way for online product companies to receive customer video testimonials, without having the ability to physically travel to each customer or client. You can ask your clients to send in 30 second cell phone videos about their favorite products and why they enjoy them. The winning video could win a complimentary product of their choice. In the invitation to submit a video, be sure to ask their permission to use their video (even if they are not a winner) in your promotional materials.

You can also ask for testimonials in your newsletters and/or any other promotional materials you send to your clients. It can be a simple addition that will make the world of difference for your business. Not everyone will respond, but if you've done a great job with your product or service, you will have selected winners who will want to help you expand and grow your business (as unofficial/official ambassadors for your company).

Example: We'd love to hear from you! If you like our [name product or service] let us know by submitting HERE what you liked best about it [provide a link to an email with the subject line filled in or some type of form to capture their quote].

If your clients submit quotes, it's always important to ask for their permission to use it any promotional materials, including the web site.

How to/where to use testimonials

Testimonials can be used just about anywhere you have a presence. This includes:

~Social media

~Print, radio, TV ads

~Newsletters

~Mailers to clients

~Your website

For examples of testimonials that have been used effectively, refer to Module 7 of the PR 101 online course at www.prformybusiness.com.

Be Creative and Have Fun with Testimonials

As you start to gather testimonials, you will generate more and more creative ways for how to use them. Your clients may even be willing to give you some ideas themselves. The good news is that your testimonials will be just as varied as the people giving them, so the type of content you receive will drive the different types of platforms you can use. Remember, you should not be afraid to use the same testimonial in different ways to reach different audiences.

Questions to Ponder:

① Are you currently capturing testimonials from your clients? If so, how?

② Who has used your product or service and has recently shared their great experience with you?

③ How can you set up a system to start capturing testimonials immediately for your business or brand?

④ Where can you strategically place your testimonials?

⑤ What creative incentives can you offer your clients to share testimonials about your business or brand to their network?

A Final Lesson...

Congratulations, you have learned the basics of PR 101! Of course, there is always more to learn on a subject, but now you know and understand the fundamentals of how to create and implement a PR strategy for your business. To recap, here are seven points to keep you on track as you build your own PR strategy and become a PR pro for your business:

◘ Identify and articulate your brand identity before creating a PR plan for your business.

◘ Pinpoint who your core audiences are that you want to engage.

◘ Determine your three to five key messages using the core C's that you want to convey to your audiences.

◘ Set goals and objectives for your plan that are in

alignment with each other and your mission.

◘ Choose PR strategies that will help you meet those goals and objectives, and select tactics to help you implement those strategies.

◘ Research and spend time with your core audiences to help establish a relationship with them, build brand loyalty, and to continue to add value to their lives and businesses.

◘ Capture testimonials from your clients, and use them strategically to build more confidence and trust in your brand.

I hope the information and guidance provided in this book was helpful to you. More importantly, I hope you implement what you have learned to further grow and build your empire. Remember, if you want a step-by-step guide with video tutorials, templates, worksheets and case studies, please visit www.prformybusiness.com to access the full PR 101 course. Happy building!

About the Author

Leslie Green is the founder and CEO of Golden Life Ventures, a communications consulting agency that combines exceptional creativity with customized communication strategies to help businesses and individuals get their brand to the masses. Leslie has implemented integrated communications and media relations campaigns that achieved the communications goals for organizations such as The Bill & Melinda Gates Foundation and the District of Columbia Mayor's Film and Entertainment Office, through the use of traditional and social media, for the past 12 years. She received a bachelor's degree in English from the University of Virginia and a master's degree in communication from Howard University.

Outside of her work as a PR professional, Leslie has a

passion for music and travel. She is a singer/songwriter and currently serves as the Creative Director for Greenhouse Entertainment, a family-run music production company, based in Washington, D.C. She also has a travel division of Golden Life Ventures, where she serves as a travel consultant. She coaches and trains others on how to break into the home-based travel arena as well. To learn more about Leslie and Golden Life Ventures, visit www.goldenlifeventures.com.

www.ingramcontent.com/pod-product-compliance
Lightning Source LLC
Chambersburg PA
CBHW061835220326
41599CB00027B/5284